ADVENTURERS

HORSEBACK RIDING

Jeremy Evans

CRESTWOOD HOUSE

New York

First Crestwood House edition 1992
© Julian Holland Publishing Ltd 1992

First published by Heinemann Children's Reference 1992,
a division of Heinemann Educational Books Ltd., Halley Court,
Jordan Hill, Oxford OX2 8EJ

Crestwood House
Macmillan Publishing Company
866 Third Avenue
New York, NY 10022

First edition

Macmillan Publishing Company is part of the Maxwell Communications Group of Companies.

Designed by Julian Holland Publishing Ltd.

Printed in Hong Kong

1 2 3 4 5 6 7 8 9 10

Library of Congress Cataloging-in-Publication Data

Evans, Jeremy.
    Horseback riding / Jeremy Evans. — 1st ed.
      p.   cm. — (Adventurers)
    Includes index.
    Summary: Discusses many aspects of horses and horsemanship, including points of a horse, popular breeds, riding techniques, safety tips, and competitive events.
    ISBN 0-89686-683-1
    1. Horsemanship — Juvenile literature. 2. Horses — Juvenile literature. 3. Ponies — Juvenile literature. [1. Horsemanship. 2. Horses. 3. Ponies.] I. Title. II. Series: Evans, Jeremy. Adventurers.
    SF309.2.E83   1992
    798.2'3 — dc20   91-23340

Acknowledgments
Illustrations: Rupert White Studio, Martin Smillie.
Photographs: *a = above, m = middle, b = below*
All photographs were taken by Sue Holland except: Cover, Kit Houghton (front), Polly Blackburn (back); 4b, Polly Blackburn; 32b, Sue Needham; 33a, Dinah Jones; 34b, Joanna Smith; 35a, S. Sparks; 45a, Zefa.

The author would like to thank Sue Holland, who took the photographs, specified the illustrations and advised on the text; secondly, thanks to the Willowbrook Riding Centre near Bosham for its invaluable help in clarifying good riding practice. Julian Holland Publishing Ltd. would like to thank the following people and organizations for their invaluable help: Jane Doust, Liz Webster, Nick Dyer, Major and Mrs Burke (Millfield School), the Mendip Pony Club and Burcott Riding School.

Note to the reader
In this book there are some words in the text that are printed in **bold** type. This shows that the words are listed in the glossary on page 46. The glossary gives a brief explanation of words that may be new to you.

Contents

Why ride a horse?

Riding a horse or pony is one of the world's great adventure sports. You take control of an animal that might be totally docile and easy to handle or highly strung and difficult. A horse is best when its behavior is somewhere in between. You have to learn to ride it and command it, and once you feel secure you can start to enjoy all the fun of riding a horse. This can be the start of a lifetime's pleasurable learning, as millions of people have found. One such is the girl in the photograph below, taking her pony over the jumps of a cross-country course in a riding club competition.

Choosing between a horse and a pony depends on getting the right size animal. Your legs must sit comfortably in the **stirrups**, and most young riders choose ponies. Ponies are small horses with easier temperaments and movements. A **hand** is used for measuring a horse's height, from the ground to the top of its **withers**. Each hand is four inches, roughly the width of an adult hand. The easiest way to measure the hands is with a marked pole. A horse starts at 14.3 hands, a pony is under that.

Points of a horse

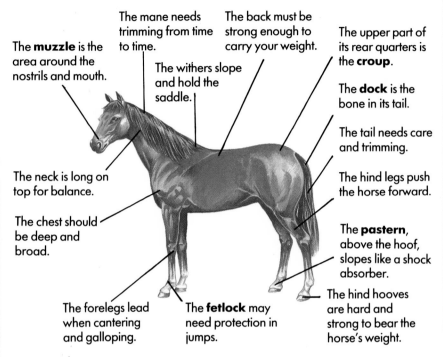

The **muzzle** is the area around the nostrils and mouth.

The mane needs trimming from time to time.

The withers slope and hold the saddle.

The back must be strong enough to carry your weight.

The upper part of its rear quarters is the **croup**.

The **dock** is the bone in its tail.

The tail needs care and trimming.

The neck is long on top for balance.

The hind legs push the horse forward.

The chest should be deep and broad.

The **pastern**, above the hoof, slopes like a shock absorber.

The forelegs lead when cantering and galloping.

The **fetlock** may need protection in jumps.

The hind hooves are hard and strong to bear the horse's weight.

TEMPERAMENT A horse or pony should behave well and be suited to your riding style. If you prefer to take it easy and go slowly, a docile, surefooted pony is the right choice for you.

AGE The life expectancy of most ponies is around 30 years. Experts say that 15 years or more is the best age for a pony to train. A pony this old has settled down. It is no longer full of youthful high spirits and is steady enough to carry young riders. For experienced riders a younger pony of around 8 years may be more of a challenge. A pony under four is unlikely to be **broken** and may be too unpredictable.

HEIGHT A pony's height must suit your height. As a rough guide, a pony should be 12 to 13 hands high for children between 10 and 12 years old, 13 to 14 hands for children between 12 and 14, and 14 to 15 hands for children between 14 and 16.

CONFORMATION This word describes how a pony is built. It affects how comfortable it is to ride, how well it takes a saddle, how much stamina it has, and whether it is surefooted.

Popular breeds

A breed such as a **thoroughbred** is a horse or pony that has been developed over hundreds of years to provide particular qualities of strength, size and speed. All breeds are recorded in a stud register. Some of the more popular ones are shown on these two pages. Horses and ponies are also described by their height, colors, markings, age and sex. For instance, a horse may be black, brown, gray, bay, chestnut, dun, roan, piebald or skewbald. Its head markings may be a star, a stripe, a blaze, a white face, a snip or a walleye. It may have white markings on its legs. A horse may be classed as a **foal**, a **colt**, a **filly**, a **yearling**, a **two-year-old**, a **gelding**, a **stallion** or a **mare**. All these terms are explained later in the book.

PONY OF THE AMERICAS
This new breed dates from 1956 and was formed by a cross between a Shetland stallion and an Appaloosa mare. This pony usually has a very distinctive light gray coat with spots of colored hair. It is a popular choice for American children.

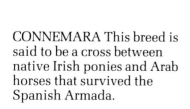

CONNEMARA This breed is said to be a cross between native Irish ponies and Arab horses that survived the Spanish Armada.

DARTMOOR The Dartmoor pony has to withstand the wild and unprotected climate of the moors of Dartmoor, in the southwest of England. It is therefore a very hardy breed and relatively small. measuring less than 12.2 hands. The Dartmoor is much prized for breeding. So is the similar Exmoor pony.

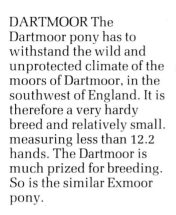

WELSH Welsh mountain ponies have lived in Wales since Roman times and have distinctive flowing manes and tails. They are well known for being strong, surefooted and friendly.

NEW FOREST PONY These ponies are found in the New Forest area in England, where they have been breeding since the 11th century. With sizes varying from 12 to 14 hands, they are sturdy and intelligent. They are considered to be excellent all-round ponies for family use.

Clothes for riding

There are a few things necessary for riders to wear. The most important is a hard hat or jockey's cap designed for riding. This cap has a hard plastic outer shell, soft foam padding inside and an adjustable chin strap. It is important that it fits well and that it won't come off in a fall.

You also need hard shoes to put enough pressure on a pony's side when telling it to go forward or to change direction. These should have heels with fairly flat soles that won't get caught in the stirrups and will come out easily in a fall. The classic high riding boots come up to the knee and are made of tight-fitting rubber or leather. They are very expensive. Many young riders may prefer **jodhpur boots,** which are short ankle boots.

Safety first

● Never ride without a hard hat. Make sure it fits well and that the chin strap is tight enough.
● Never ride in soft shoes, shoes with deep-ridged soles or shoes without heels.
● Never carry glass bottles in your pockets or anything that could break or hurt you in a fall.
● Wear gloves for a firm grip on the reins.
● Take waterproof clothes if there's any chance of wet weather.

Jodhpurs

Jodhpurs are the best kind of riding pants because they're tight fitting and strengthened on the inside. Ordinary jeans tend to ride up your legs. Then when you grip the sides of the pony the **stirrup leathers** can pinch your legs. Elasticized jodhpurs are much more comfortable and are easily washable.

The rider on the left is wearing cream-colored jodhpurs together with jodhpur boots. She is correctly dressed for a cross-country competition, following the rules and regulations set down for riding. For this she has a quartered silk cover on her hat, together with matching shirt and string gloves.

Dress and turnout

A T-shirt, sweater and windbreaker are suitable clothes for riding. Most serious riders, though, feel that an efficient rider always makes an effort to look as neat and tidy as possible. The traditional styles of riding clothes are shown below for **dressage** and **hacking**. The jackets are waisted and flared with slits at the back so that they hang properly. They are designed so that you look attractive when sitting in the saddle. Apart from hunting red, riding clothes are usually neutral colors, plain tweeds or black or dark blue for senior riders. You can also add to this outfit a cravat, and if you belong to a riding club, an official tie and badges.

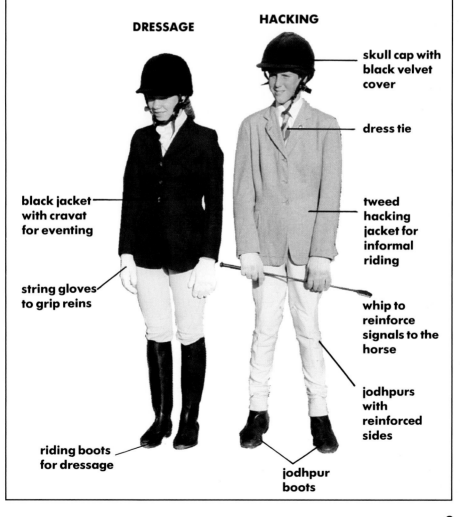

DRESSAGE

HACKING

skull cap with black velvet cover

dress tie

black jacket with cravat for eventing

tweed hacking jacket for informal riding

string gloves to grip reins

whip to reinforce signals to the horse

jodhpurs with reinforced sides

riding boots for dressage

jodhpur boots

Horse sense

Extra protection

You can injure your back or head if you fall off a horse or pony. While the riding cap will hopefully save your head, the back protectors shown on the left are essential additions to your clothing when you start jumping. The most popular one is shown here. It is a lightweight jacket that is heavily padded down the back, with a rigid panel to protect your spine. You can wear an ordinary jacket over the top of it.

Safety first

● Always ride with others.
● Tell someone where you are going and when you expect to be back.
● Ride only where you know it is allowed.
● Close all gates behind you.
● Avoid damaging crops or disturbing cattle or other animals.
● On a long ride you should stop and give your pony a drink and a rest. As you come to the end of the ride, it is usually best to walk the pony so that it arrives cool.

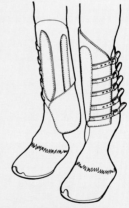

The pony may need protection too. These boots are designed to protect its legs from cuts and bruises when jumping fences and walls in the countryside.

Safety on the road

If a horse or pony is to be taken on roads, it must have steel shoes fitted by a blacksmith to protect its hooves. With regular use, these will need to be changed every four to six weeks. You can read more about blacksmiths on page 42.

The first rule of riding on the road is to wear bright clothing that can be easily seen. The second is to take your pony on the road only if you know you can control it in traffic. Keep to a walk or a slow trot so that there is no chance of slipping.

Always ride on the same side as the traffic. If possible ride on the grass shoulder. When riding in a group, the first and last riders give the road signals. You should signal in good time, sticking your arm out to the left if you are turning left, and to the right if you are turning right. If you're going to stop, wave your arm on the road side up and down. If necessary, you may need to stop a car to cross a road, though only do this when it is not dangerous. Hold your hand up, look directly at the driver and cross when he or she has stopped for you.

If there is something unusual ahead that is likely to frighten your horse or pony, wait until there is no traffic before you ride past it. If necessary, get off and lead the animal past. Try to avoid riding at night or in fog. If you ride in the dark, you must wear reflective clothing and use stirrup lights that show red behind and white in front.

When cars slow down, pull out or stop for you, give them a wave and thank them so that they'll do the same for other riders and for you next time this kind of thing happens.

11

Tack

Tack or **saddlery,** is the name for the saddle you sit on, the **bridle** that controls the horse and the other pieces that riders need, shown in the photograph. The reason you need a saddle is that most people can't ride bareback, because it is slippery and uncomfortable. You need a bit, bridle and reins to control a horse.

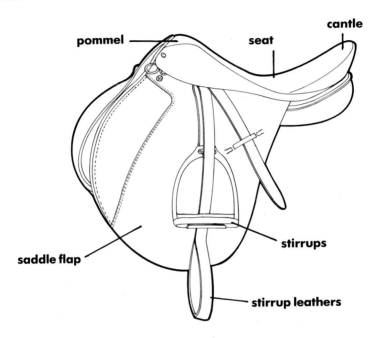

Guide to the saddle

Usually, saddles are made of leather stretched over a wooden frame, which is called a **tree.** Wool, felt or foam rubber are used as padding. A proper leather saddle is very expensive to buy, but with the right care it will last for many years of hard use. You can also buy saddles made from synthetic materials. The purpose of the saddle is to spread your weight correctly over the pony and to allow you to sit in the correct position for riding. To be absolutely perfect, a saddle should be made specially to fit you, but this is not necessary so long as the fit is reasonably good. Before you buy a saddle you need to fit it to the pony. There is a pad of quilted cotton or fleece placed under the saddle to protect it from dirt and grease. This liner also makes it more comfortable for the pony. A **girth** is the wide strap used to fasten the saddle around the pony.

The bridle

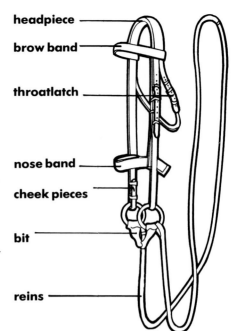

headpiece
brow band
throatlatch
nose band
cheek pieces
bit
reins

The bridle is also made of leather. It is made up of straps that are secured around the horse's head. The **nose band** is attached to the **headpiece**, **brow band** and **throatlatch** by the **cheek pieces.** The cheek pieces hold the **bit** in the horse's mouth. The bit is made of steel or rubber and is used to control the horse. A soft rubber bit is said to be mild and is used for a horse that is easily controlled. Thinner steel bits are called severe and are used to control stronger, more highly strung horses.

The **reins** are attached to the bit where it joins the cheek pieces. They give the rider control by pulling on the horse's mouth.

Caring for your tack

The saddle should be treated with care. Carry it with your forearm underneath. You can then carry the bridle in your hand or on your shoulder, leaving one hand free to open doors. If all this is too heavy, carry it with both hands. When you put the saddle down on the ground, stand it on the pommel to protect the tree. Leave the saddle out of the way, so it won't be kicked or damaged by the horse.

Your saddle and bridle should be washed down after every ride if they're muddy. Otherwise clean them at least once a week. A wet sponge will remove mud and dust from the saddle and bridle. You can clean them with saddle soap. Finally, dry polish them with a cloth. Regular oiling will keep the leather supple. If you don't do this, they will dry out.

Horse questions

Q: What is a **snaffle bit**?
A. The bit is the metal or hard rubber part of the bridle. It fits into the horse's mouth over its tongue. A snaffle is the simplest kind of bit and should be used for all young horses and ponies. If a pony gets too strong or hard mouthed for the snaffle, an experienced rider may change to the **double bridle bit**. This bit helps the rider control the horse more exactly. The third main kind of bit is called the **Pelham bit**, which also uses a double bridle.

Looking after it all

Check all your tack carefully for wear and tear. Stirrup leathers, reins and other parts of the bridle can all break under strain. Replace them if necessary as quickly as you can. For proper cleaning, you have to take the saddle and bridle apart. Once cleaned, the parts can be put together again.

When cleaning tack, wear overalls to protect your clothes or wear old clothes. Use a sponge for washing.

Apply saddle soap and oil your saddle regularly. Wash the stirrups and clean them with metal polish.

A snaffle bit, cheek straps, brow band, throatlatch and headpiece, grip reins, stirrups, saddle and leather girth strap are laid out for inspection.

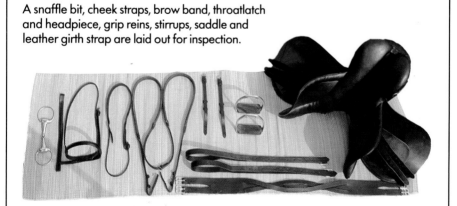

Getting to know a pony

Caring for your own pony takes a great deal of time. You need to know how to look after it, and you need the time to look after it. You also have to have enough land to stable it and keep it in a pasture.

Never go into a paddock alone, unless you are used to a pony and it is used to you. First, you must get to know it. Talk to it. Walk up to it and stroke its nose or pat the sides of its neck to make friends. Horses and ponies like to be given tidbits. Beware, though, because too much makes them inclined to nip people with their teeth since they will always be expecting food. They like sugar lumps and candy, but as with humans, these are bad for their teeth.

Never forget your pony. You should walk it, handle it and talk to it every day.

Markings

● A star is a white mark on the forehead of a horse or pony.
● A stripe is a narrow white stripe on the forehead.
● A blaze is a broad white stripe on the forehead.
● A white face covers forehead, eyes and some of the muzzle.
● A snip is a white mark between the nostrils.
● A sock is a white mark covering the fetlock.
● A stocking is a white mark covering the leg beneath the knee.

Walking your horse

If your horse or pony is used to being walked every day, there will be no problems. The **halter**, or head collar, is like a simple bridle that is used to hold the pony. Call it and walk up to it with the halter behind your back. If there is a gate, be careful to close it behind you. Slip the lead rope over its neck and catch it on the other side so you have it firmly. Then put the halter on. Give your horse a pat to thank it. You can then take the lead rope and say "Walk on!," which is the first command you give your pony.

Walk at the pony's shoulder and learn to lead it from both sides. You should be able to see the halter, which holds the pony's head, as you lead it along.

Never pull backward on the lead rope to try to make a pony walk. It will really dislike this and probably dig in its feet and refuse to move.

Safety first

● Always wear a hard hat when mounting a horse or pony.
● Check that the girth is tight enough.
● Always keep hold of the reins with at least one hand.
● If you're unsure, ask someone to hold the bridle for you when you mount.

● Always keep the ball of your foot on the **stirrup iron**. Never let your foot go right through the stirrup, or it may get caught. Wearing boots with solid heels helps prevent this.
● Always close the gate when going into a field or paddock with a horse or pony.

Putting on the saddle and bridle

When you are ready to put on the saddle and bridle, use the lead rope of the halter to tie the pony to a suitable ring or other fastening. Use a **quick-release knot**. Go to the side of the pony and put on the liner, then the saddle, sliding it down the pony's back. Catch hold of the girth, which is hanging down on the far side, join it to the near side and tighten up the buckles. The pony may not like this and may blow out its chest while you're doing it. This means you always have to check the girth strap when you're up on the saddle, and tighten it if necessary. To remove the saddle, push the stirrups up to the top of the stirrup leathers, undo the girth strap and lift the saddle off.

Next you must fit the bridle. Undo the buckle on the halter and slip it down the pony's neck so that the pony is still tied up.

To fit the bridle, first put the reins over the pony's head. Carefully push the bit into its mouth while you slide the headpiece over its ears. Check that the straps and bit are level. Tighten the nose band and finally tighten the throatlatch, which should be loose enough to allow your hand to fit between it and the pony.

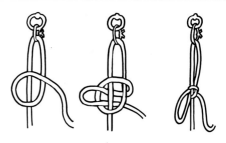

The quick-release knot, with a safety loop that pulls it open, should always be used for tying up a horse or pony.

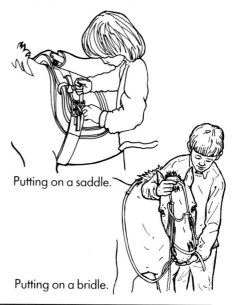

Putting on a saddle.

Putting on a bridle.

Horse types

- A bay horse has a reddish brown body with black mane and tail.
- A chestnut horse is ginger.
- A gray horse is all gray. This can be iron gray if it is more black, or white gray if it is more white.
- A dun horse is a brownish dark gray, with black mane and tail.
- A roan horse is a mixture of brown and gray or black and gray.
- A piebald horse has large patches of black and white on its body.
- A skewbald horse has large patches of white and any color except black.

Mounting

2. (Below). Put the ball of your left foot into the stirrup. Jump up, holding onto the saddle with your right hand. Take care not to kick the horse with your left foot.

3

1. (Above). Always get on, or mount, from the left side of the horse, facing back toward the tail. Hold onto the reins and the horse's mane with your left hand. Steady the stirrup with your right hand.

2

3. (Above). Straighten your left leg and swing your right leg up and over to the other side. Be careful not to kick the horse as you do this.

Dismounting

1

2. (Below). Hold onto the front of the saddle with your right hand and swing your right leg up and over, still holding the reins.

3

1. (Above). To get off, or dismount, first take both feet out of the stirrups. Keep holding onto the reins and lean forward, with your left hand holding the horse's mane.

2

3. (Above). Slide down the horse's side. Then you can lead it by the reins with the stirrups pushed to the top of the stirrup leathers. Never leave a horse saddled for long while not riding it.

In the saddle

Once you're up in the saddle, you should check the girth. It should be tight enough so that the saddle won't slip to one side when you move off. If possible get someone to tighten it for you. You can do it yourself, though, by moving your leg forward and lifting the saddle flap to get at the buckle. If the saddle has slipped around while you were trying to mount, you must take it off the horse and put it on again.

The stirrups will probably also need shortening or lengthening so that your legs are comfortably bent when in the saddle. Take one foot out at a time and adjust each stirrup leather so that the stirrup iron, the horizontal base of the stirrup, is about level with your ankle. Stand up in the saddle to check that it feels right.

You should sit in the middle of the saddle, with your knees and thighs ready to grip the saddle flaps. Look ahead, keeping a straight back with your shoulders held back and elbows by your sides. Hold the reins so that they form a straight line from your elbows to the bit, with your hands just above the withers.

It is extremely important to hold the reins properly, as shown here. Gloves provide the necessary grip on leather reins and should be worn whatever the weather.

Balance exercises

Before beginning, it's worth doing exercises, such as those shown below, in the saddle to help get used to what may seem a strange and uncomfortable position. Ask someone to hold the horse's head if you are not sure that it will stay still. Other exercises that you can do with your feet in the stirrups are swinging your arms from side to side, touching your toes, leaning right back and standing up in the saddle.

Always sit upright on a horse or pony, keeping a straight back. The stirrups should be shortened so that your legs are comfortably bent. When learning it's a good exercise to ride without the stirrups at a walk and a **canter**. This helps you get your balance and produces what is called a **deep seat**. When doing this, always cross the stirrups over the saddle to avoid annoying the horse.

Good exercise for getting your balance in the saddle is leaning forward and lifting yourself on the stirrups to touch the horse's ears. While doing this, always keep one hand on the reins.

Lungeing

Lungeing is a way of exercising a horse while someone else controls it. The horse moves around in a circle on a lungeing rein. This exercise can be used in training horses. It can also help an inexperienced rider get used to the movement of being in the saddle with someone else in control of the horse. The lungeing rein is attached to the bridle by a **swivel clip**, so the inexperienced rider doesn't have to hold the reins. The instructor must be very experienced. He or she holds the lungeing rein in one hand and a whip in the other, while giving the horse commands.

Know your horses

- A **foal** is a newborn horse.
- A **colt** is a male up to three years old.
- A **filly** is a female up to three years old.
- A **yearling** is in its first year after birth.
- A **two-year-old** is in its second year after birth.

- A **gelding** is a **castrated** male.
- A **stallion** is an uncastrated male.
- A **mare** is a female.
- A **cob** is a big-bodied, short-legged horse or pony no higher than 15.2 hands.
- A **mule** is a cross between a donkey stallion and a pony mare.

Aids to control your horse

In the photograph below, the rider is giving a light kick with her feet against the sides of the pony and telling it "Walk on." These are natural aids, which are signals from the rider to the horse that tell it what to do. The aim is that it understands clearly and responds immediately. Natural aids are the legs, the hands, the seat and the voice.

A squeeze with the legs behind the girth tells a horse when to go faster, turn or move sideways. At the same time the hands holding the reins are used to control and guide the horse. Never pull on the reins too tightly or the horse will soon ignore everything that you ask it to do. Moving your weight in the saddle is another aid that can help direct the horse.

You also use your voice to control your horse. Keep your commands simple, and the horse will soon understand words such as "Walk on," "Trot," "Steady" or "Halt." It will soon get used to the tone of your voice. You can then use different tones to praise the horse, scold it or calm it down when necessary.

The two artificial aids used by experienced riders are a whip and spurs. The whip is not used for whipping the horse. It's for giving it a light tap on the **quarters**, to add to a leg aid that has been disobeyed. Normally the whip is carried and used by the inside hand, the hand that is on the inside of a turn. Standard whips are made of leather or fiberglass.

Changing pace

Horses have four paces. These are the walk, the **trot**, the canter and the **gallop**. Aids are used to increase or decrease the pace. Changes from walk to trot, trot to canter, or canter to gallop, should be as smooth as possible.

The speed of the pace will depend on the pony or horse. Obviously there is a great difference between a racehorse and a Shetland pony. However, in all cases the aids are similar, if not the same.

Walk to trot

Start off on a walk by lightening the pressure on the reins, kicking gently with your legs and saying "Walk on."

When you are ready to increase the pace from a walk to a trot, shorten the reins, as the horse will shorten its neck. Give the horse the necessary aids by kicking with your legs and saying "Trot." At first you can sit in the saddle, changing to a **posting** or **rising trot** once the horse has set up a steady rhythm.

Trot to walk

The pony shown above is trotting. To slow down from a trot to a walk, sit down in the saddle and press down with your backside. Pull gently on the reins to put the brakes on and give the command "Walk." At the same time use your legs to keep the horse moving straight, taking care you are not bounced forward as the horse slows down. As soon as the command is obeyed, loosen the reins slightly.

24

Riding at a walk and a trot

The walk is the slowest, most comfortable pace. Each hoof hits the ground separately in a 1-2-3-4 rhythm – first the nearside foreleg **1**, then the offside hind leg **2**, then the offside foreleg **3**, and last the nearside hind leg **4**. As the horse walks, its head bobs up and down. To allow for this you must hold the reins very lightly. Remember they are to control the horse and not for you to hang on to. If you do not feel secure, keep a hand on the saddle or mane until you get the feel of it. Sit upright. Don't lean forward or look down. To stop the horse, push down with your backside, give a little more pull on the reins, close your legs against the horse's side and say "Halt."

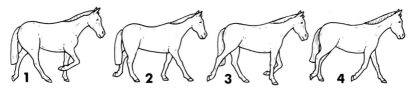

The trot is a faster, 1-2, 1-2 pace. The horse's hooves hit the ground in pairs – the nearside foreleg and offside hind leg together **1** and **2**, and then the offside foreleg and nearside hind leg together **3** and **4**. It is a bouncier and altogether less secure feeling than walking, and you should be confident at walking before you increase the pace to a trot. Sitting down is the easiest but least comfortable way to trot. It is much better to rise up and down in time with the pony's movements. This is called posting or rising trot.

Posting

Allow the bounce of the horse's stride to push you up from the saddle, leaning forward very slightly to keep balance. Then sit back down in a regular rhythm that matches that of the horse. To help, you can count "1-2" or "Up-down" in time with the beat of the front hooves. Keep your back straight and your hands and lower legs still. Posting is a knack that may take some time to learn. You need to be able to do it, though, before you move on to the next pace.

25

The canter and gallop

The canter is a 1-2-3 pace with either foreleg leading. If the offside hind leg leads **1**, the nearside hind leg and offside foreleg follow together **2**, then the nearside foreleg **3**, and then the offside hind leg **4**. It's an exciting pace, which you should only try when you can handle the trot properly. Although it's fast it's much smoother than the trot and allows you to sit in the saddle. The trick is to not let yourself be bounced around. You should use your back, hips and seat to absorb the movement of the horse. When cantering around a corner, the horse's inside leg must lead.

The gallop is a 1-2-3-4 pace, though at one stage all four hooves are off the ground. If the nearside foreleg leads **1**, the offside hind leg follows **2**, then the nearside foreleg **3**, then the offside foreleg **4**. This is the fastest pace and only experienced riders should try it. If you intend to gallop you can shorten the stirrups so that you can lift your weight off the horse's back and onto the balls of your feet on the stirrups. This leaves the horse free to move as it wishes. The most extreme riding style is used by racing jockeys who ride on very short stirrups. They throw their upper bodies forward over the horse's head for maximum speed.

Stopping a gallop

Galloping can be dangerous and may take you by surprise. If you feel that your horse is about to take off from a fast canter, slow it immediately by pulling in the reins firmly but gently, relaxing them and pulling them in again until the horse obeys. Sit back in the saddle, keeping your legs still by the horse's side. If you can't slow it down, try turning it into a circle and make the circle tighter and tighter until it slows down.

The gallop lets the horse cover the most ground with each stride, stretching out its legs and head as far as possible.

Changing direction

You need to learn how to turn a horse to the right or left when riding at any pace. The horse must be able to bend its body evenly, making an arc around the turn. It must keep its balance and rhythm, with the outside hind hoof following the same line as the outside front hoof.

To turn a horse to the left, you should pull lightly on the left rein while loosening the right rein a little. Press your outside leg, the right leg, against the horse's side to stop its hind quarters from swinging out of the turn. Your inside left leg acts as a turning point for the horse. Keep sitting square to the saddle, but allow the horse to look into the turn by bending its neck. Do exactly the opposite for a right turn.

The jump

Jumping a horse over a fence or other obstacle is very exciting. Once you are confident with a walk, trot and canter you can start learning to jump. A jump is divided into the approach, takeoff, jumping through the air, landing and recovery.

APPROACH AND TAKEOFF
Learning to jump is much easier with an experienced horse. Before you start, shorten your stirrups so you can get into the jumping position with your weight over the horse's center of gravity.

You need to start the jump correctly, with the horse facing the jump straight on. Jumping from an angle should be avoided by all but experts. If your approach is correct, the jump will normally be successful. The horse knows when to take off. It will fold its forelegs and push off on its hind legs with its head stretched out. As it does so, you should lean forward to give it plenty of rein and avoid pulling on its mouth.

THE JUMP AND LANDING As you fly over the jump, you have to grip the horse tight with your legs and keep your body close to the saddle. The horse folds its hind legs to clear the jump. You must sit back down in the saddle to absorb some of the impact as its forelegs hit the ground. Its hind legs follow, as you take over control for a smooth landing.

A jump taken correctly with the rider looking ahead to the next one.

Perfect or failed jump?

Falls are to be expected when jumping. They are normally due to an incorrect approach to the fence or obstacle. At the last moment the horse hesitates and decides it won't jump, and the rider is thrown over its head. All you can do is hang on and try to stay in the saddle.

28

Jumping in stages

Practice for natural jumps, such as fallen trees or ditches, by trotting your horse over large poles. Walk the horse over them to start with, so that it gets used to lifting its feet to clear them.

When the horse has learned to adjust its stride to clear the poles at a walk, you can approach them at a posting trot. Let your hands go forward to allow the horse to stretch out its head and neck, but keep light contact on the reins. As you and the horse become more experienced, try trotting over poles that are more closely spaced.

The next stage is to trot over a raised pole about 8¼ feet away from the last flat pole. The traditional way of raising poles is to use **cavalletti**. These are poles or crosspieces that were used by the Italian cavalry. Nowadays, many riding schools have found it safer to use blocks.

As you become more experienced, you can approach raised poles at a canter. This is more difficult. A typical mistake is to confuse the horse by accidentally tugging on the reins as it begins its jump. To stop yourself from doing this, practice trotting over poles without holding the reins.

29

Away from home

Traveling

The pony above is dressed for travel in a horse trailer. It wears foam-padded boots to protect its legs against getting injured in the closed-in space of the trailer, a tail bandage to protect its tail and a traveling blanket to keep it warm. Most trailers are open at the front and are therefore drafty. You must cover the horse with a heavyweight blanket in winter so that it is warm enough.

To load a horse into a trailer, look straight ahead as you hold its halter and lead it up the ramp. Secure the safety strap behind the horse and tie the halter with a quick-release knot to the front of the box.

Hacking

Hacking is the word used for going out for a ride in the countryside. If you are hacking with a party from a riding school, the horse will almost certainly know the way better than you. If you leave it to do what it wants, it will wander along slowly on the way out but will suddenly increase its speed in a mad dash close to home. So be sure to keep control to make it go where you want, when you want. You are the rider, not a passenger.

Horses are surefooted animals, but they may need some help going uphill and downhill. When riding up, take your weight off the horse by leaning forward. This allows it to push more freely with its hind legs. When riding down lean backward a little. Unless a hill is very steep it's usually best to head straight down the hill, to prevent any chance that the horse will slip and slide. Always follow the tracks and, if in doubt, dismount and lead it at a walk.

As a break from schooling, a party sets out for a hacking trip in the hills.

Safety first

● Always use a quick-release knot to secure the halter in a horse trailer.
● Make sure the box is well padded.
● Give the horse hay to keep it happy.
● Only allow your horse to go with a careful driver.
● Stop and check the horse on a long trip.

Trekking

Trekking is going out for a long ride in the countryside and may involve crossing wild areas. If the trek lasts more than a day, you will have to arrange overnight stabling. This usually needs to be pre-booked. There are many tour operators who organize treks in interesting areas. They will provide the route, the horses and the accommodations.

Equipment can be carried in a saddle bag or backpack and should include extra clothing, food, drinks, maps and a compass. Always trek in company and tell someone where you are going and when you expect to be back in case of possible problems.

Competitive events

Dressage

Dressage is taken from the French word "*dresser*," which means to train. Dressage is a series of maneuvers for the horse and its rider. Many times it is done in competitions. Judges mark these movements with a score ranging from 1 to 10. These may include walking, trotting and cantering at different paces, as well as **pirouetting** over a certain distance. The horse and rider are also marked for impression, calmness and obedience, position and seat.

Show jumping

Show jumping consists of riding over a set series of closely spaced fences in an **arena**. In most competitions the rider with the fastest round of clear jumps wins. If the crossbar of the fence doesn't fall off, the jump is counted as clear.

Show jumping is held at every level. Top class international show jumping has now become big business. It is often televised, and the riders are full-time professionals who earn large amounts of money.

Eventing

Eventing is a series of tests. It is often reckoned to be the most challenging test for a horse and rider. Best known are the three-day events, which start with dressage and finish with show jumping. Eventing also includes speed and endurance tests and a cross-country section. The scores on these events count more heavily.

SPEED AND ENDURANCE This is divided into three parts. To start, the riders have to cover about 4 miles of roads and tracks at a steady pace. Next, they ride a **steeplechase** course, which is usually done at a very fast gallop. Then, there is more riding on roads and tracks before the cross-country course.

CROSS-COUNTRY The cross-country course imitates conditions in the country. The riders have to cross a series of obstacles such as ditches and jumps. They are marked on how fast they complete the course. Unlike those used in show jumping, the crossbars of these jumps are fixed and cannot be knocked over. This makes them much more dangerous for the horse and rider.

Gymkhanas

Mounted games, called **gymkhanas,** started in India where **polo** ponies were used at first. Gymkhanas are competitive, fast-moving events. These games appeal to young riders who want something less formal than show jumping or eventing. Nevertheless a gymkhana pony needs to be properly trained to cope with the excitement and the risks of a gymkhana course. The games that rider and pony have to tackle may include collecting potatoes in a bucket or bareback jumping.

Polo

Polo is played on horseback with a mallet, a ball and two goals. It started in ancient Persia and became popular in India. From there it passed on to the British who helped introduce it to the rest of the world. The first Westchester Cup between England and the United States was played in 1886. There are two opposing teams with four people to a side. Each game is divided into **chukkars** of seven and a half minutes. Since polo requires nonstop galloping a fresh pony is needed for each chukkar. This helps to explain why polo is one of the world's most expensive sports.

Long-distance riding

This is the competition version of trail riding. A special route over rough country is divided into stages. Each stage must be completed within a set time, with the horse in good condition. Its pulse and breathing are checked, and if it is judged not fit to continue the rider must withdraw. At a steady trot a top horse and rider can complete 93 miles of a long-distance event within 15 hours. Shorter events may take place over two or three days. To succeed at long-distance riding, both rider and horse need hard training to toughen the horse's legs, build up stamina and improve pace.

Driving

Driving is a competitive event in which horses or ponies pull a wagon or carriage. The carriage can be driven by a single horse. Two horses are known as a pair, and four are known as a team. A one-up carriage takes a single driver. A two-up carriage takes a driver and groom and is called a tandem. Four-in-hand carriages belonging to the coaching class will take three or four people. Running a four-in-hand carriage such as a **phaeton** with a team of top horses such as Austrian Lippizaners is a sport for the very wealthy. A simple tandem, though, can be driven by Shetland ponies. Driving competitions at the international level are intense.

There are usually three stages of a three-day event. Presentation and dressage come first. A trotting and walking **marathon** comes next. This involves some fast driving over hazards such as deep water, a sand pit, railed fencing and steep slopes. Finally there is obstacle driving, in which the carriage has to be driven around closely spaced cones.

Riding schools

You can't teach yourself to ride. Even when you have your own horse or pony there's always more to learn. You will need lessons. A riding school or equestrian center is the place to do this. It must be an approved establishment that will guarantee you properly qualified instructors, a wide choice of well-looked-after horses and ponies, good equipment and high safety standards with proper insurance against accidents. If it's situated in pleasant surroundings, so much the better.

Choosing a school

You might want to go to a riding school that someone has recommended to you, or you can visit a few schools and then make a choice. Ask to have a look around before you decide which will suit you best. Find out about the sizes of classes, the availability and cost of individual teaching, and the type of riding you will be able to do. Also ask about facilities for more advanced activities such as dressage or show jumping. Many schools offer intensive introductory courses for beginners over five or seven days. After that they give regular lessons. Schooling, which is the term used for learning in a closed area, should be balanced with hacking trips for variety. The school should also teach you how to look after horses, with stabling, grooming and keeping them in a pasture.

The riding arena

An arena is an enclosed riding area for schooling. If you live in a cold climate it should ideally be indoors to use in the winter. An outdoor arena that is floodlit and has good drainage, though, may serve as well.

The arena is usually around 130 feet long by 65 feet wide. It is marked out with letters that you can follow in a set pattern. This allows you to practice and learn exercises that involve turning the horse — called changing the rein — at a walk and at a trot. For instance, you can ride in diagonals and squares, in large circles and small circles, and in figures-of-eight. Or you can follow a twisting course that takes you back and forth across the arena. Riding in such a restricted area can become a little dull, and it is important to alternate it with hacking.

Your own pony

An ideal situation, from left to right: horse stall, tack room and two **loose boxes.**

Stabling

Owning your own horse or pony means you will need somewhere to keep it. You can keep a pony in a pasture all year long with a field shelter, or at a stable which is the equivalent of a horse hotel. You can also keep it in your own stable, in its own stall.

Most horses only need stabling in the winter. Then they need to be taken out for regular daily exercise. Every day you will also have to **muck out**, and to water, feed, groom and cover the horse with its rug and blankets as necessary. Keeping a horse is a time-consuming job that demands total dedication and involes responsibility.

Mucking out is an essential chore.

Mucking out

Mucking out, or cleaning, is a daily chore that should be completed first thing in the morning. The horse needs clean bedding. This is usually made of straw or wood chips. You have to pick out the horse's droppings with rubber gloves and remove any wet straw.

A full muckout is needed at least once a week. Put the cleanest straw or chips to one side, remove the rest and brush out the stall. Let it dry out if possible. Then re-lay the old bedding and mix in new bedding. You will find a pitchfork, shovel, hard brush and a wheelbarrow useful. Ideally the floor of the stall should slope toward a drain. This will make mucking out easier.

Keeping in a pasture

Keeping a pony outdoors is easier and cheaper than stabling, though you should still pay a daily visit. The main disadvantage is that you need a large enough field of around one acre per horse or pony.

The field should be enclosed with a post and rail fence, and a padlocked gate that also has a secure catch. There must be a continuous supply of clean water to drink. If your horse is to be left out all year some sort of shelter may be necessary in colder climates. A pony with a thick coat can stand very cold weather. A pony with a thinner coat should be given a waterproof, fitted rug, known as a New Zealand rug, during the worst of the winter.

Feeding

Grass is a natural food for horses. Hay, which is dried grass over six weeks old, can be fed to them in a stable using the hay net shown here. This should be hung from the wall, so the pony can pull out a mouthful as it wishes. The hay should be crisp and sweet smelling. If it's musty or moldy, throw it away.

Apart from a regular supply of hay and water, a pony should have extra food if it is being worked. If it is being worked hard, this should be three feedings a day. The first would be at around 8:00 A.M., the second following exercise at around noon and the third at around 5:00 P.M. when you close the stable for the night.

A feed is made up of energy foods so the horse can exercise, and bulk foods to fill it up. Typical energy foods are barley, oats and corn, while bulk foods include sugar pulp, chaff, and bran.

Cleaning and grooming

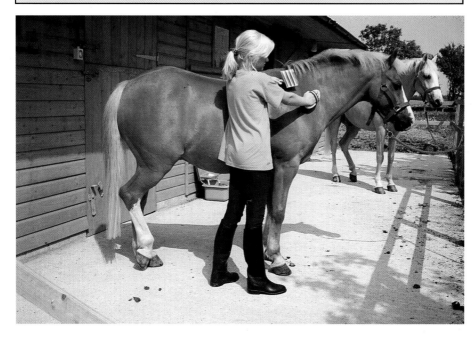

A horse that spends most of its life outdoors needs only light cleaning. Brush it down to remove mud and sweat marks, and to keep the tail and mane tidy. You can also sponge its eyes, nose, muzzle and dock. Grease and dandruff do not need to be brushed out of its coat as they contribute to the horse's natural waterproofing.

A horse that is stabled requires regular grooming, which is called deep grooming. It's a tiring job, and a proper groom will take up to 45 minutes, cleaning and massaging the horse's skin to keep it fit and healthy. If a horse is left ungroomed, the owner's neglect will soon become obvious.

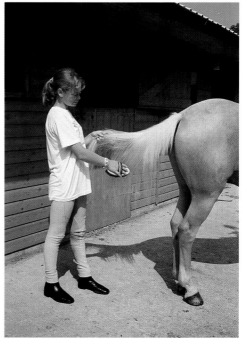

Grooming a pony's tail with a body brush removes dust and dandruff.

Plaiting

For the dedicated rider, grooming never stops. A plaited mane to show off the horse's neckline is necessary for dressage and is widely used for show jumping. The tail can also be plaited.

Tools for grooming

- A body brush is to clean dust and dandruff from the coat, mane and tail.
- A curry comb is for cleaning the body brush, or to clean mud from a horse kept in a pasture.
- A dandy brush is to clean heavy mud and dust from a horse kept in a pasture.
- A hoof pick is for picking stones out of hooves.
- Hoof oil is for oiling hooves.
- A stable sponge is for cleaning eyes, nose and muzzle. A different sponge should be used for cleaning under the tail.
- A stable rubber is for a final polish of the coat.

Foot care

A horse should have its feet attended to regularly. Small stones and anything else that may be embedded there should be picked out. The hoof pick is used for this. Work on each leg in turn. Facing backward, run your hand down the horse's leg from the shoulder to the fetlock, and pick up the hoof. Use the hoof pick to remove anything lodged in the foot, working from the heel to the toe. The sensitive underneath of the hoof is called the **frog**. Be careful not to push the pick into it. Check that the shoes are secure and in good condition. Dry hooves can be treated with hoof oil, which is painted on with a small brush. This gives the hooves a shiny appearance and helps keep them from cracking, which is uncomfortable for the horse.

Use a hoof pick to clean the hooves.

The blacksmith

"No foot – no horse" is an old saying. You need to take care of a horse's hooves. The blacksmith, or **farrier,** plays a big part in doing this.

If a horse goes on roads frequently, its hooves will wear down faster than they can grow. They therefore need to be shod with steel shoes in the well-known horseshoe shape. Generally a horse with shoes should be checked by the blacksmith once a month. Even if the shoes don't need replacing, the hooves may have grown outward and will need reducing. This is done with a rasp, or file, with the shoe removed. If this is neglected the horse could become severely lame.

Check regularly to see if shoes have been lost, have come loose or have worn too thin, and also that the hooves are not overlong or out of shape.

The blacksmith uses a tool called a **buffer** to loosen the nails holding the old shoe, which is pried off.

He trims the hoof with clippers and a rasp, then presses the red-hot shoe onto the hoof so that it molds to a perfect fit.

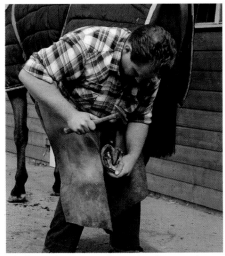

Nails are hammered into the shoe, and a rasp is used to trim the sharp points that stick through. This doesn't hurt the horse.

Checking a horse's health

A healthy horse looks alert with pricked up ears, wide open, bright eyes and a glossy coat that lies flat. It shouldn't sweat when not moving unless the weather is very hot. It should eat well and chew regularly. Your horse should stand evenly on its legs and take strides of equal length. These are some of the things to look for when you make your daily inspection. Other signs of a healthy horse are pale-colored urine and regular droppings like damp balls.

A horse must be regularly fed and watered to keep it healthy, and be given treatment for worms every six weeks. It should be inoculated as advised by the **veterinarian,** or **vet**, who will also check the state of its teeth. A specialized horse vet will usually come to you when called. The vet has to deal with many problems such as colic and **laminitis** caused by poor feeding and eating too much rich grass, as well as bad cuts and cracked heels.

Horse questions

Q: Can I treat my own horse?
A: Build up an **equestrian** first aid kit and learn to heal small cuts and cure other minor problems.
Q: What do I do if my horse becomes lame?
A: Do not ride the horse. If you are riding, you must get off immediately. You can tell if a horse has become lame because it lifts the lame leg and drops its head on the other side. Check the hoof for a stone or sharp thorn, and use a hoof pick to remove it. If lameness continues, do not ride the horse but walk it to the nearest phone and call the vet.

The Pony Club

Pony Clubs encourage young riders, up to the age of 21, to get the most from their ponies. The Pony Club was formed in Britain in 1929. Similar clubs are found in the United States, Canada, Australia and New Zealand. Their addresses are on page 46.

Pony Clubs are divided into local branches that organize many events, with trained instructors on hand. Regular rallies cover road safety, stable management or gymkhanas involving mounted games. Competition meetings include show jumping, cross-country, dressage, polo and tetrathlon, which includes shooting, swimming, running and riding phases.

Pony Club events are fun. Above is the Mendip Prince Philip Team, while below young riders examine a tail bandage.

Famous riding schools

The Spanish Riding School, Vienna.

Most countries with a strong riding tradition have important national horseback riding centers. Probably the most famous is the 300-year-old Spanish Riding School, which, despite its name, is in Vienna, Austria. This school is thought to teach the highest levels of formal horsemanship that exist. It uses the famous Lippizaner stallions and gives public demonstrations in the art of advanced horsemanship.

The French equivalent to the Spanish Riding School is called the Cadre Noir. It is in Saumur, close to the River Loire. It has stabling for 450 horses, and arenas for show jumping and dressage, as well as cross-country and steeplechase courses.

The US Equestrian Center in New Jersey trains riders to the highest levels so they can participate in international competition.

Horse questions

Q: How long does it take to learn to ride?
A: It takes years to become really good. You need to have a good sense of balance, a liking for horses, the will to learn to ride properly and a certain amount of courage. You must be taught properly. The more eager you are to learn, the quicker you will improve.

Remember that horses are animals. You can never know exactly how they will react, so there is always some uncertainty and risk in learning to ride them.

International associations

The Australian Pony Club
PO Box 46
Lockhart
NSW 2656, Australia

The British Horse Society & The Pony
  Club
The British Equestrian Centre
Stoneleigh, Kenilworth
Warwickshire CV8 2LR, UK

Canadian Pony Club
RR1, King City
Ontario LOG 1KO, Canada

Irish Pony Club
Knocbawn, Kilmaconague
Co Wicklow, Eire

New Zealand Pony Clubs Assn
Kaitieke, RD2 Owhango
King Country, New Zealand

South African Pony Club
109 Ninth Street, Parkmore
Johannesburg 2196, South Africa

The United States Pony Clubs
125 Weaver Street
Greenwich, CT 06831 USA

Glossary

arena: an area for events such as show jumping or dressage
bit: a bar of metal, held in the horse's mouth, to guide and control
bridle: the leather straps that hold the bit in the horse's mouth
broken: a horse is broken when it accepts a rider for the first time
brow band: part of the bridle – the strap over the brow
buffer: a tool for loosening the nails of a horse's shoe
canter: a fast pace between a trot and a gallop
cantle: the back of the saddle
castrated: with the testicles removed
cavalletti: a series of timber bars for teaching jumping
cheek pieces: the bridle straps that fit down either side of the horse's head
chukkar: a period in a game of polo. Several chukkars make up a match
cob: a big-bodied, short-legged horse

or pony under 15.2 hands
colt: a male horse or pony up to three years
croup: the area behind the horse's back, over its back legs
deep seat: the art of sitting firmly in the saddle, particularly on a canter
dock: the bone in the pony's tail
double bridle bit: this consists of a loose-ring snaffle bit, a curb bit and a curb chain
dressage: the movements and maneuvers of horsemanship
equestrian: anything to do with horses
farrier: a blacksmith who shoes horses
fetlock: the area behind the horse's leg, above its heel
filly: a female horse or pony up to three years
foal: a horse at birth
frog: tender inner part of horse's hoof

gallop: the fastest pace

geldings: geldings are stallions that have been castrated, making them more docile and easier to ride

girth: the wide strap that fastens the saddle to a horse

gymkhana: a local horse meet with mounted games

hacking: riding out in the countryside

halter: the head collar used to secure a horse in place of a bridle

hand: measurement of height used for horses. A hand is about 4 inches

headpiece: leather strap that buckles onto the cheek pieces and allows the length of the bridle to be altered

jodhpur boots: short riding boots often with straps or elastic sides

jodhpurs: trousers for riding

laminitis: inflammation of a horse's hoof

loose box: a stable where horses run loose

lungeing: riding in a circle on a long rein

marathon: a long-distance event

mare: a female horse

muck out: to clean out a horse's stall

mule: a cross between a donkey and a pony

muzzle: the area around the horse's mouth

nose band: the leather strap that holds the bridle around the horse's nose

pastern: the area in front of the horse's leg, above its hoof

Pelham bit: a type of double bridle bit

phaeton: a lightweight open carriage

pirouetting: an advanced dressage movement that involves the horse turning in tight circles

polo: an equestrian sport played with mallets and balls

pommel: the front of the saddle

post: to rise with each forward step of the horse's outside leg

quarters: the part of the horse directly behind a rider's lower legs

quick-release knot: a knot that can be undone very quickly. It can be used for tying up a horse

reins: the straps held by the rider, connected to the bridle and bit

saddle flap: the flap on either side of the saddle, which covers the girth straps and sweat flaps

saddlery: the saddle, bridle and all that goes with them

seat: how you sit on a horse. Sitting correctly is termed having "a good seat"

snaffle bit: a metal bit suitable for most young horses and ponies

stallion: an uncastrated male horse

steeplechase: a race over fences, which originally finished at a church tower

stirrup: either of a pair of D-shaped metal or leather foot supports hanging down from a horse's saddle

stirrup iron: the frame carrying the rider's foot

stirrup leathers: the leather straps attaching the stirrups to the saddle by means of the stirrup bar

swivel clip: a clip used to attach a lungeing rein to the bridle

tack: horse's equipment, also **saddlery**

thoroughbred: a horse bred for racing

throatlatch: the leather strap that holds the bridle around the horse's throat

tree: the wooden frame of a saddle

trot: the pace between walking and cantering, either a sitting trot or a posting (or rising) trot

two-year-old: a horse in its second year

veterinarian, or **vet:** a horse or animal doctor

withers: the area where the neck of the horse meets its back

yearling: a horse in its first year

Index

The numbers in **bold** are illustrations.